IMAGES OF ENGLAND

Castle Cary, North Cadbury and Wincanton

T0353182

This cart was made by Squibbs at Station Road, Castle Cary for the Frome United Breweries Co. Ltd of Bruton. The breweries registered office and main depot was at Vallis Way, Frome.

IMAGES OF ENGLAND

Castle Cary, North Cadbury and Wincanton

Sam Miller & Bridget Laver

NONSUCH

Bruton High Street, 1947. On the left is the shop of A.E. Amor & Sons, stationers.
They also had a 'circulating library', seen advertised in the window. Next is the premises
of Powell and Rossiter, motor engineers, who had another depot at the Glen. The large
building to the right is the Congregational church built in 1803.

First published 1997
This new pocket edition 2006
Images unchanged from first edition

Nonsuch Publishing Limited
The Mill, Brimscombe Port,
Stroud, Gloucestershire, GL5 2QG
www.nonsuch-publishing.com

Nonsuch Publishing is an imprint of Tempus Publishing Group

ISBN 1-84588-258-X

Typesetting and origination by Nonsuch Publishing Limited
Printed in Great Britain by Oaklands Book Services Limited

Contents

Introduction   7

1.   Towns   9

2.   Villages   41

3.   School Days   65

4.   Pastimes   79

5.   At Work   107

6.   Personalities   121

Acknowledgements   128

The market place, Wincanton. The town had a new water supply in 1848 when this stone pump (complete with lamp) was erected in the Shambles in the Market Place. The cost was just a little over £56. The pump was removed in 1879. On the right is the Red Lion which has stood here for over 200 years, and above that the old town hall.

Fore Street, Castle Cary, 1932. On the left is the shop once owned by Appleby's and then, from 1940, by Mr and Mrs Spearman who ran it as a toy, wool and stationery shop. The Ashman's took over until 1985 when the premises became a pet shop run by Mrs Maureen Higgins. On the right in 1858 was Ellis, the confectioners. At the end of the nineteenth century Wosson Barrett had taken over the premises having the only wine licence in Castle Cary. Messrs Real and Holton took over after that and then Sparks who made a duplicate of Princess Elizabeth's wedding cake in 1947. For a while it was Wheadons cafe before the Co-op moved here from across the street. Further up the street was John Coleman's drapers shop. Mr Coleman was reputed to have built the house. It was a drapers shop until 1980. Green and Company were here in 1896, then E.C. Webber, Joe Tullett and Tom Trowbridge. Since 1981 it has been the Bailey Hill bookshop. Next door was B.W. Bellringer, the coachbuilder. Mr Wells turned it into a garage and Jack Norris took over until retirement in 1969. Since then it has been a hardware shop, firstly Overt Locke and latterly Dave Marsh.

Introduction

Photographs of south-east Somerset rarely make the pages of general guide books on our county. We don't know why, for this part of Somerset is full of history, tradition and legend. In this book we hope to redress the balance, as we visit the market towns of Castle Cary, Bruton and Wincanton and a host of villages, each one with a character of its own. The photographs illustrate town and village scenes of 'yesterday' as well as people at work, at play and at school. They have been brought together by Bridget Laver and Sam Miller who have lived in the area, Castle Cary and North Cadbury respectively, all their lives.

Advertisement for E.J. Parker, 1965.

One

Towns

Fore Street, Castle Cary. A view reproduced in 1912 from a photograph taken in 1858 which showed the many changes that had taken place in just fifty years. The first shop shown was Gosney's cycle shop and had been a grocers. Next came a private house in 1858 and Clifton Thomas boot shop in 1912. Then came a printers shop, previously a chemist both run by the Moore family and then Mrs Coles, a dressmaker. These four buildings occupy the site of the Phoenix Inn yard and were built after 1829. After Mrs Coles in 1858 came George Hicks, a shoemaker and then some private houses. In 1912, Mr Barrett's confectionery premises was run by a Mr Ellis by whom it was built. In 1858, Mr Wosson Barrett's grocery shop was then a thatched cottage occupied by John Stadden who was a basket maker. Mr Charlie Butt bought the house and pulled it down and built the present house and shop. In 1912 the next shop was a pork butchers, previously occupied by Arthur Clothier, a shoemaker.

The Prince of Wales public house on Bayford Hill, Wincanton, c. 1912. This inn had previously been called the Rising Sun and Bayford Hill as either Sunny Hill or Conduit Hill. The Prince of Wales was demolished in 1935 as part of a road-widening scheme. Also seen here are the arms of Stavordale Priory.

Sexeys Hospital in High Street, Bruton. Hugh Sexey was born at Bruton in 1556. He became one of the auditors of the exchequer, which office he held until his death in 1619. Sexeys Hospital was founded in 1638 and was endowed with the Manor of Blackford (near Wedmore). It provided lodging and maintenance for eight old men and women, although this number has fluctuated over the years. Both Sexeys School at Bruton and Sexeys at Blackford were founded from the endowments of the hospital.

Right: The Carmelite Priory and Roman Catholic church in South Street, Wincanton. The modern-day Catholic church was founded in Wincanton in a cottage in North Street. In 1881 the congregation purchased Acorn House and stables in South Street. During the following year the Carmelite Order arrived to take charge. By 1889 a new priory was built which became the centre for training novices in England in 1902. It was used as a Red Cross Hospital during the First World War. Acorn House was demolished in 1908 and the new Catholic church of St Luke and St Teresa was built.

CARMELITE FATHERS,
ST. LUKE'S PRIORY, WINCANTON

Below: The Wincanton Union Workhouse. The site for the new workhouse at Wincanton was chosen in March 1836 and was purchased from the representatives of the late John Brown for £300. The foundation stone was laid on 29 March 1837 and the builder was Mr Davis of Langport. The cost was £3,550 and all the bricks used were made on site. The first relieving officers were Henry Legg for Wincanton, Uriah Phillips for Bruton and James Sims Bord for Castle Cary. A regime of poor diet and hard work was the order of the day. Married couples were separated and the inmates dressed in a uniform with the initials of the wearers home parish sewn on the back. Harry Burton and his wife, Dove, celebrated far and wide as the 'King and Queen' of the Gypsies, ended their long lives here. Dove died in February 1846 aged 95 and Harry in July 1847 aged 94. Both were interred in Wincanton churchyard. By the 1930s the workhouse had become 'Town View' a home for the elderly, but the stigma of being in the workhouse was still a reality. This photograph makes the building look almost like a country house with the well-kept gardens in front. The building was finally demolished in 1973 and the site now forms part of the West Hill housing development.

Cumnock Terrace, Castle Cary. This terrace of twelve houses was built in 1877 by John Boyd and was named after his birthplace in Scotland. The houses were intended for employees of his horsehair factory in the town.

The butchers shop in Fore Street, Castle Cary. This property previously belonged to a Mr Powell. William Taylor who had a shop in Frome married Ida Pitman, a niece of Mr Powell (they are on the left of this photograph) and on his suggestion the Taylors came to Cary and traded as butchers under the name of Powell. Their steers were kept in fields now covered by Millbrook and Victoria Park housing estates. Mr Taylor also ran the London Central Meat Co. situated in the Triangle. Bill Derrett was also a butcher here and then Messrs Asher and Vaux who owned Castle Cary Bakeries bought the premises and opened a bread and cake shop. They sold to Dikes of Stalbridge who sold to Keinton Mandeville Bakeries.

Bruton, May 1937. In a competition run in Bruton as part of the Coronation celebrations of King George VI and Queen Elizabeth in 1937, this car won the prize for the best decorated private car. The vehicle belonged to Mrs E. Jones who owned a drapers shop in the High Street. Mrs Jones, who was a member of the organizing committee also won a silver cup for the best decorated shop front.

Bruton floods, 12 July 1982. Over four inches of rain fell on Bruton on Monday 12 July 1982, accommpanied by thunder and lightening which brought wide-spread flooding to the town. The force of water was so strong that it carried four cars with it which ended up in a private garden. This scene is at West End and shows the flood water rushing through the streets.

High Street, Wincanton, 1926. William Loud was a butcher here in the High Street at Wincanton who took over from James Lock. The lane next to his shop and leading to his slaughterhouse was known for some years as Louds Lane. When he died he left the business to two members of his staff, Messrs Harvey and Harris. They carried on for a few years, then the premises were sold and demolished. On the open space was later built a new police station and library in what is now called Carrington Way.

The Dolphin Hotel, High Street in Wincanton. This public house and hotel was once known as the Rainbow Inn. In 1774 the landlord was William Hervey. By 1794 the name had been changed to the Daulphin and was occupied by Robert Bessant. However it soon became known as the Dolphin and has remained so for the past 200 years. One previous tenant drowned himself in a tank of water and another diversified into the bakery business. This photograph taken in 1900 shows a variety of carts for hire. The little cottage immediately next door now houses the Wincanton Town Museum.

The Britannia, Castle Cary. This inn possibly received its name in 1805 when Cary raised a corps of volunteers to prepare for the threatened French invasion. The name 'Britannia' would have appealed to the patriotic townspeople. After the first landlord, John Dunford, his place was taken by his son-in-law, John Speed Andrews. Three men of this name followed each other here. During the whole time the Andrews family were here the patriotic character of the house was maintained. The Union Jack was often flown outside and ceilings and walls were decorated with loyal and patriotic emblems. In 1875 it was described as a Commercial Inn and Posting House, carriage and fly proprietor, good loose boxes and lock-up coach houses available and parcels agent, by appointment to the Great Western Railway company. Another landlord, Samuel Herman lost his life in the *Titanic* disaster of 1912. The name has now been changed to the Horse Pond Inn.

West End, Bruton, 1982. This is the aftermath of the floods which devasted parts of the town on 12 July 1982. These cars were washed down stream by the force of the water and ended up here in a private garden.

Squibbs Garage, Station Road, Castle Cary. John Frederick Squibb, grandfather of the late Chris Squibb was both landlord of the Heart and Compass and founder of the coachbuilders, wheelwrights and undertakers business. The firm changed with the times as the horse was superceded by the internal combustion engine. The Heart and Compass stayed with the Squibbs until 1952. The new showrooms for the garage business were built in 1930 and the whole premises demolished in 1987 for a new housing development.

Bruton High Street, 1937. The premises of Mrs E. Jones photographed on the morning of 12 May 1937. Mrs Jones won a silver cup for the best decorated shopfront in the town in a competition arranged as part of the celebrations for the coronation of King George VI and Queen Elizabeth. Other events arranged for the same day included a carnival parade, childrens and adults sports, community singing and a dance with the Denver Club Dance Band. The dove cote was floodlit for the occasion.

Right: The Round House on Bailey Hill, Castle Cary, a national monument. It was built from funds made available from the parishes of Castle Cary and Ansford and bears the following inscription, 'This Round House (one of only four in the country) was built in 1779 by Wm Clark for £23 (from local charities) as a temporary prison or lock-up. It is 7 feet in diameter and 10 feet high with two iron grills for ventilation. In 1894 it was repaired as a result of a shilling subscription and in 1922 the Lord of the Manor, Sir Henry Hoare Bart JP, presented it to the parish'.

Below: Hutchings of Wincanton. Mr F. Hutchings opened a fruit and veg shop in the High Street in Wincanton before the First World War. He also grew flowers and had a large nursery and greenhouses nearby. This photograph was an advertisement for his flower arranging.

Left: An unusual view of Fore Street, Castle Cary. It was taken in 1984 from the top of the Market House and looks towards the junior school in the top right hand corner. Judging by the lack of shoppers it was probably a Sunday morning. The sign of the George can be seen in the bottom right hand corner.

Below: Fore Street, Castle Cary, showing the stream that used to run down the right hand side of the road, *c.* 1950. The van on the left belonged to J.L. Fennon whose shop was then next to the White Hart.

Wincanton. A more modern photograph of the town. On the left is the White Horse Hotel which dates back to the mid-seventeenth century when Robert Vining was the landlord. He was succeeded here by his son, John in 1655. Mrs Dickory was the landlady in 1678 and she in turn was succeeded by another John Vining and then by George Dean. The house was rebuilt in 1733 by Nathaniel Ireson. In the next century after a long succession of landlords some of whom were owner/occupiers, the premises was opened as a wine and spirit merchants. On the right is the Bear Hotel which was badly damaged in a fire in 1718 and was put up for sale. It was approved to be sold to innkeeper Richard Pouncett for £95. Mr Pouncett could not raise the money and the sale was cancelled. In 1720 the inn was rebuilt and by 1730 the owners Edward Pouncett and Samuel Laver leased the property to John Webb who was here for almost 40 years. In the 1840s, a Thomas Grist was landlord and the hotel became a very popular place for both locals and travellers. It was said that a dozen or so coaches stopped here every day. However, this trade was soon to be lost with the coming of the railways.

Ottons, Station Road, Castle Cary. Ralph Otton established his business in Station Road, Castle Cary in 1908, as a complete house furnisher, selling blinds and rollers, bedsteads, carpets and rugs, perambulators and push cars. Picture framing was a speciality and upholstering, repolishing and repairs were undertaken. Ralph built the premises himself.

Coylton Terrace and the old Toll House, Wincanton, c. 1900. Coylton Terrace was built about 1830 by a Mr Linton, a Scotsman by birth. In the latter part of the nineteenth century Mrs Elizabeth Drover ran a private ladies boarding and day school here. (There were two other ladies schools and also a commercial boarding school, all of which were in High Street). There were gates across the road here at Bayford Hill and also across the top of Common Road (on the right of the picture). The gates were purposefully high so that a horse could not jump over. 'Road rage' must have been evident when the gates were in place, especially when flocks of sheep or herds of cattle were on the move. The gate was only opened wide enough to allow one animal through at a time to be counted and the toll worked out. The toll house itself used to have an angled front on which was a board exhibiting the tariffs. The turnpike trust was abolished in 1874.

The Market Place, Castle Cary. The Market House, on the right of the picture, was built in 1855 on the site of an old brick building. It provided a convenient place for the sale of agricultural and other produce. The ground floor was mainly for the sale of fresh food, meat, cheese and butter with farmers and farm factors operating in other parts of the building. It has also been used as a police station complete with cells, a theatre, town council offices, for dancing classes and as a tourist information centre. Here the ground floor is used to display an assortment of farm machinery and tools. Notice the unattended horse ambling along the road. The Angel Hotel (formerly known as the Catherine Wheel) is in the centre of the picture. This property dates from at least 1786. Since the closure of the inn the premises has been used for a variety of purposes. The George Hotel and Worlds Stores complete 'the square'.

Opposite: Wincanton High Street, 1930s. On the right is Uncle Tom's Cabin, which was opened as a public house by Thomas Green in May 1861. It was named as a direct result of the American Civil War which started in April 1861, ten years after Harriet Beecher Stowe's book of the same name. Further down the street on the same side are Frisby's shoe shop, Dowdings grocery store and White's bakery and tea rooms, all of which have gone. Opposite Uncle Tom's Cabin is the Dolphin Hotel.

Above: The Town Hall, Wincanton, 1901. There was a town hall or market house here about 220 years ago but it was in a very ruinous state. A new market house and town hall were built in 1769 at a cost of £400, it was enlarged in 1867 at a further cost of £800. On the west side of this building was the town 'lock-up' known as the Blind House because the only light came from a grill in the door. More than one prisoner died here. Before much of the £800 could be paid off the town hall was destroyed by fire (1877). The damage was estimated at £1,600. The new town hall was opened in October 1878 and at the same time the road was widened and the new tower was erected. Insurance recovery was £800 and another £400 was raised by subscription. Several concerts were held and the debt was soon cleared. Further alterations took place in 1893.

Left: Laver's Shoe Shop, Market Place, Castle Cary. Pithers occupied these premises at the beginning of the twentieth century as part of their furniture emporium. By 1908 Edwin Harris of Wincanton had started a branch of his boot and shoemaking business here. He was taken over by Frank Laver who died in June 1935 leaving many debts. His son, Hubert Frank Laver then took over the business with the help of Mr Willoughby Wyatt. Mr Laver eventually sold to Parkers who already owned the next door premises. Mr H.F. Laver is seen at the door of his shop, c. 1937.

Station Road, Castle Cary (previously known as New Road). The Somerset and Dorset Joint Railway Parcels Receiving and General Enquiry Office in Station Road. The horses and carriage belonged to Jim Weeks. The nearest station to Cary on the Somerset and Dorset line was Evercreech Junction. The parcels office was later transferred to the White Hart in Fore Street when Mr Weeks took the licence of that public house.

Above: the Market Place, Castle Cary. On the right is the George Hotel which dates from the middle of the seventeenth century. Tradition has it that stone from the castle ruins was used in the building of this house. Thomas Cox was the first recorded landlord and the fashionable game of 'sword and dagger' was often played here. By 1788 George Pew was not only the landlord but ran the local post and excise office from here as well. In 1845 the brick part of the building was rebuilt after a disastrous fire. The George was also the parcel office for the Great Western Railway and 'omnibuses' from here met trains at Cary Station twice daily in the years before the First World War. The shop on the left with the canopy is that of E.J. Parker and Son. Mr Edward Parker started his tailoring business in his home in Florida Street in 1888. He later moved to the Market Place when these premises were vacated by Charlie Pither who moved to the High Street. Later Parkers moved next door where John Pither had his furnishing business. Parkers later took over the shop that had been used by Mr Close as a saddlers and opened a ladies department. The company has now been trading here for over 100 years. Parkers have also had branches at Wincanton and Bruton. Further up the street the printing works and stationers of J.H. Roberts can be seen. This shop has also been run as an electrical shop by Fennons and by Tuckers of Wincanton and more recently has been the premises of Wincanton Carpets. Also seen is the bank, Stuckeys from 1856 to 1909, then Parrs, the Westminster and now the National Westminster.

Left: the Market Place, wincanton,1903. This is the premises at number 11, the Market Place, Wincanton of Mr George Sweetman. Sweetmans was a stationery warehouse, publishing office and bookshop. Many of the books were of particular interest to the people of Somerset, Dorset and Wiltshire and many were in dialect. Mr Sweetman published his monthly illustrated journal from here. He also wrote the history of Wincanton and many smaller booklets about the town and surrounding area.

The Dogs, Tout Hill, Wincanton, c. 1901. On Wednesday 26 November 1688, Prince William of Orange (later King William III), marched with his own guards and attended by a great many of the gentry of Somerset and Devon through the West Country. On arriving at Wincanton he lodged at the home of Richard Churchey, a merchant of the town. In 1688 Richard Churchey lived at 'The Dogs', a house which had only recently been built. It was then known as 'The Manor House'. Churchey was lord of the manor and owned about 500 acres and several houses and cottages. He died in 1697. The house was restored by Nathaniel Ireson in 1740 and the name 'The Dogs' was first recorded in 1805. It was named because a stone dog stood on each of two pillars at the entrance. The room where the Prince of Orange slept became known as 'The Orange Room' and in that room are some paintings produced by French prisoners of war who were lodged here from 1805 to 1815.

South Street, Wincanton, 1890. The alleyway between these buildings is now the entrance to Balsam Fields. The large thatched house (a farm house?) was demolished in 1891 and replaced almost immediately by a pair of Victorian villas. The house with the lamp was pulled down in the early 1920s and the alleyway widened into a road.

Jubilee cottages, Ansford Road, Castle Cary. These five pairs of cottages were built for John Boyd in 1887 by C. Thomas and Sons at a cost of £1,047. They were given to the town for the use of the aged poor who were to live rent free and receive an allowance of six shillings a week from a trust fund. The cottages were named in honour of the Golden Jubilee of Queen Victoria. They were demolished in the 1970s. The original tenants were, Philip Wade, Eliza Pitman, Elizabeth Paul, Jane Kick, William Noble, George Jefferies, John Eaton, Maria Wright, William Holland and Mary Ann Cave.

Fore Street, Castle Cary, 1937. The best dressed shop premises in Castle Cary on the morning of 12 May 1937, the coronation day of King George VI and Queen Elizabeth, was that of Wosson Barrett & Co. Sidney and Wosson Barrett started business in what is now the Co-op in about 1880 as Barrett Bros., trading as cooks, caterers and confectioners. They later expanded further up into what is now Tom's Place, Hospice Shop, Pandora's Box and the opticians, as pork butchers and grocers. The partnership was dissolved in 1904 and Sidney carried on in the original shop with Wosson taking over the rest. Sidney died in 1919 and Wossons' eldest son Robert William Herbert Barrett took over Sidney's business. Wosson died himself in 1930 and his son, Wilfred took his place in the shop. The business lasted until 1939 when it went bankrupt.

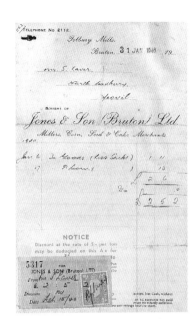

Advertisement. Jones & Son of Tolbury Mills, Bruton, 31 January 1940.

The Greyhound, Wincanton, 1925. The Greyhound was one of the principal inns in the town and was built in c. 1710. Tradition has it that the body of the Duke of Sussex laid here and that Queen Victoria spent a night here when a child. After the opening of the railway an 'omnibus' from the Greyhound met every train. The premises lay semi-derelict for some years but the courtyard complex seen here in 1925 has, in the last few years, been converted to mews cottages.

No. 33 High Street, Wincanton. Budgens garage otherwise known as Ireson garage was opened by Thomas Budgen in 1917. He was succeeded by his son, Harold who retired some 30 years ago. The family also had premises at No. 28, trading as motor and cycle engineers, iron, zinc and tinplate workers.

Miss Mead's Cottages, South Cary, 1905. These cottages in South Cary, sometimes referred to as the Almshouses or Swiss Cottages were built at the expense of Miss Mead the daughter of a former vicar. They were let rent-free to poor 'widow-women' of Castle Cary and were built on the site of the parish pound in mid-Victorian times. The parish pound, sometimes called the pinfold was then re-sited in South Cary Lane but by 1900 had not been used for many years. Previously the pound had been near the horse pond. The cottages are now privately owned. The photograph also shows the Arms of Cary.

The Triangle, Castle Cary, c. 1910. Goups of children pose for the camera by the horse pond at Castle Cary. The premises occupying the corner site was Brakes Coffee Tavern and Dairy Shop and before that it was a private house. It is now the Chinese takeaway. Next door on the right looking up Fore Street, was a sweet shop run for many years by Mrs Woods and for a short time by Maureen Higgins. Before becoming Cary C.B. and Photographic Centre it was an antiques shop. The first large building in Fore Street on the same side of the road is the White Hart Hotel. Originally occupied by William Bulgin who was a cabinet maker by trade, the White Hart was opened as a public house by John Marshall in 1836. At one time there was an open ditch running down this side of the street and the house could boast of a front garden and fence. By 1846 James and Thomas Marshall were running the business. The house was restored and a new front was added in 1872 and the inn had changed hands five times by 1890. During the time that Jim Weeks was landlord, the White Hart was the parcels receiving office for the Somerset and Dorset Joint Railway.

Church Street, Wincanton, 1929. Looking towards the parish church of St Peter and St Paul. In the churchyard is the tombstone to the potter Nathaniel Ireson. He designed it himself and it includes his effigy. He died in 1769. Wincanton parents used to tell their children that when Nathaniel heard the clock strike midnight, he came down off his pedastal to drink and then went back again and although many tried to see this feat no one succeeded. The thatched dwelling on the right of the picture was formerly three cottages. It was converted to one home in the 1930s. The building below that (with a glass dome over its porch) is Lambrook House, once the office building for the Wincanton Transport and Engineering Company. In 1905 this was a private boarding and day school for girls with Miss K.C. Fowler as its headteacher. Just prior to the Second World War the school had become co-educational, but closed soon afterwards.

The Somersetshire Bacon Curing Company, bill head for 1911. The Bruton Bacon Factory (a branch of South Western Dairies) was at Vineys Yard at Bruton and was opened in 1899 on the site of a former silk factory. A large number of Bruton men were employed here. Note the telephone number, very easy to remember. During the Second World War local families who fattened a pig in their garden, brought them here for slaughter. They were allowed to keep only half the pig, the rest went to the war effort.

The Isolation Hospital, Dancing Lane, Wincanton, c. 1920. The Wincanton Isolation Hospital and Sanatorium was built in 1910, it is better known today as Verrington. The first hospital in the town was opened in 1901 in the High Street. By 1922 this was thought to be quite inadequate and a house was purchased and equipped to the highest standards. Also in the High Street even this was soon out of date and a purpose-built cottage hospital was opened in Balsam Park in 1932. It was named the Wincanton (East Somerset) Memorial Hospital and the opening ceremony was performed by H.R.H. Princess Alice, Countess of Athlone.

Right: The Abbey Wall, Bruton, 1914. In 1142 a priory was built by William De Mohun for the brotherhood of Black Canons, on the ruins of a Benedictine monastery. The abbey was granted by Henry VIII to his standard bearer, Sir Maurice Berkeley in 1546. Charles I visited in 1641 and again in 1644. The Great Hall of the Abbey House was burnt down in 1763 and the rest (except this wall) in 1786. This card was posted in Bruton at 8 p.m. on 5 January 1914 to Miss Doris Hill at Castle Cary from her mother, and read 'If I can I will come tomorrow afternoon'. Such faith in the postal system and only a $\frac{1}{2}$ d stamp. (You could buy 480 $\frac{1}{2}$ d stamps for one pound in those days).

The Abbey Wall Bruton

In 1142 a Priory was built by William de Mohun for the brother hood of Black Canons, on the ruins of a Benedictine Monastery. The Abbey was granted by Henry VIII to his standard bearer, Sir Maurice Berkeley, in 1546. Charles I visited Bruton in 1641 and again in 1644. The Great Hall of the Abbey House was burnt in 1763, and the rest was pulled down in 1786.

Below: Cliff House, Bruton, 1952. Cliff House was once a private house in the occupation of John Crouch Christopher. It later belonged to Mr F. Stroud who sold it to the visitors of Sexeys Hospital. In 1892 Cliff House was opened as a boarding house for the boys of the new Sexeys Trade School which had just opened. It was enlarged to meet the growing demands of the school in 1929.

Above: Castle Cary. At the Horse Pond on the morning of 25 April 1908 someone was ready with their camera. Was this weather expected, we doubt it. The pavements are already being cleared with plenty of spectators on hand to offer advice. In the background is the elegant spire of the parish church. The postcard was sent on 5 July 1908 and informs that Mr J. Donne at the Mansion is dead. This is almost certainly John Stephens Donne of Florida House, Castle Cary.

CCY.58 THE COBBLES, CASTLE CARY

Left: The Pitchings, Castle Cary. The Pitchings is a cobbled pathway running down between the Market House and Chinns antiques shop. At the bottom and across the road can be seen the premises of T. White & Sons, Ironmongers. This building was re-fronted in 1804 when Anthony Nancolas, a clockmaker bought the house and commemorated his marriage to Ann Tidcombe by rebuilding, incorporating their initials and the date. Thomas White established his business here in 1883 (it had previously been a candle factory). Still trading under the same name over 100 years later it is now run by Mrs Celia Wheadon and her sons.

Cow & Gate, Wincanton. This factory was owned by the West Surrey Central Dairy Company Ltd in 1919 in an area of Wincanton known as the Tything. It became known as Cow & Gate in 1929 and merged with United Dairies Ltd in 1959 to become Unigate. The whole complex was demolished in the mid 1980s.

Westminster Bank, Wincanton. At about 2 o'clock in the morning of 15 May 1944 a bomb fell on the Westminster Bank in South Street. It destroyed the bank, the offices of solicitors Dyne, Hughes and Archer and the home of Miss White. The bank manager's daughter was the only fatality.

Bruton Church and Bridge.

Above: Bruton Parish Church, 1920. The parish church at Bruton, dedicated to St Mary was re-built towards the end of the fifteenth century. It is said to be one of the finest examples in the country of the early perpendicular style. It is unique in having two towers, the smaller one acting as the north porch. The two cottages on the right of the picture appear to be derelict and were pulled down many years ago. Note the steps going down to the river, in days gone by the river was used to dispose of waste material of all kinds, the river water was also used for drinking and cooking.

Left: Fore Street, Castle Cary. The shop front of grocer 'Tinker' Phillips (seen here). His wife was well known for the faggots she used to make. The property belonged to Joe Tullett who then rented to S.J. Phillips until he could find out premises of his own. Phillips grocery business then moved to Regent house leaving this as a hardware store. More recently this was 'Sporting Image' and is now the Cary Cobbler.

Right: North Street, Wincanton, *c.* 1910. This cycle was on loan from the Wincanton Carnival and was used as an advertisement aid. It is outside Arthur Tucker's cycle depot in North Street in an area of the town known as Shatterwell. Tuckers cycle business was next to Wincanton County Police Station.

Below: Mill Street, Wincanton. This street was at one time the main thoroughfare through the town and has not changed greatly in the last 100 years. The Congregational church and the Baptist church were both in Mill Street. The Congregational church closed its doors for the last time in 1960 but the Baptist church is still in existence; it was started here in 1832. At the bottom of the street is Town Mill which was demolished in the 1960s.

The May Fair, Bailey Hill, Castle Cary. From a copy of a drawing dated 1 May 1884. A charter was granted by King Edward IV whereby a market could be held weekly on Thursday, with fairs on the eve, day and morrow of St Phillip and St James and also on St Margaret's Day, which is 1 May and 20 July. Another charter was granted in 1614 for a market within the town every Tuesday and a fair on the Thursday before Palm Sunday. There was at this time a flourishing sheep market at North Cary. The markets were later held at Millbrook. In 1809 Castle Cary market was referred to as one of the best in the West of England, there being nearly 600 head of cattle. There were later four fairs held every year. The first was known as 'Little Weaving Tuesday' and was the day when the weavers and cloth workers had a 'day out'. The last of the four was known as the 'Gibbet Fair', in memory of Jack White. The annual show of the East Somerset Agricultural Society was held at Cary every third year, this honour being shared equally with their neighbours, Wincanton and Bruton.

Woodville Street, Castle Cary, 1906. This is now known as Woodcock Street and the first building on the left used to be Hunts Bakery and is now Barrington Antiques. Further along is Montague House with the veterinary surgery behind and then Woodville House (it kept its name when the street name changed). This house was the site of the first Barclays Bank in Castle Cary. It was also the family home of the Talbott family who ran a tobacconist and hairdressers business opposite. The large building in the centre of the photograph was the old Boyd Institute built in 1885. It later became the Liberal Club and has had many uses in the last 40 years.

Opposite: Castle Cary Methodist Church. The foundation stone for the Methodist church was laid on 26 June 1838 and the opening services were held in May 1839. The hut on the right was Gyngell's photographic studio, built by Monty Squibb's father. During some very rough weather in 1905 it was blown into the road and damaged beyond repair. The cart on the left belonged to the railway company.

Left: South Street, Wincanton. This is the temporary premises (looking very South-American in design), of the Westminster Bank built after the bomb which had destroyed the original building in 1944.

Below: North Street, Wincanton. The old National School was built at the top end of North Street in 1838 and was used for educating the children of Wincanton until 1896. Many of the houses here are of seventeenth century origin and in one, Roman Catholic services were held in the 1880s. On the left is the old county police station, built in 1856 and used as such until 1973. Next door was the site of the first Congregational church in the town.

North Street, Wincanton. 5029

Right: Woodcock Street, Castle Cary. Irene Talbott and her father stand outside their tobacconist and hairdressing shop. In later years Rene and her brother Jack traded as hairdressers under the name of Jarene from the same premises. Mr Talbott senior started his hairdressing and tobacconists with his sister in what is now 'The Changing Rooms' on Bailey Hill. At that time there was a small room on the side where Mr Talbott used to keep a barrel of cider. The farmers would cycle up for a haircut on Saturday nights and then have a glass of cider.

Below: Advertisement for G.F. Benjafield's shop at Wincanton.

Wincanton Priory.

Left: Wincanton Priory. The interest in this photograph of the interior of Wincanton Priory lies on the reverse. It was sent in February 1915 from Wincanton to Mr Henry Lambrecht, a Belgian refugee staying at Horsington. It includes the message 'Vive la Belgique'. It was found by chance at an antiques fair in Belgium in October 1996 by Bridget Laver.

Below: Squibbs Garage. Kath and the late Chris Squibb at their garage premises in Station Road, Castle Cary, shortly before it was sold for housing development in 1986.

Two

Villages

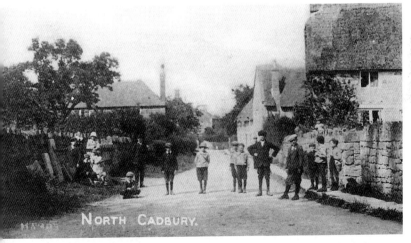

NORTH CADBURY.

High Street, North Cadbury, c. 1910. Not so very different from today. Looking closely there are at least 18 children posing for the camera. The house on the right lost its thatched roof in 1970 when it was replaced with tiles and there are gates at the entrance to what is now the village hall car park.

Above: Holbrook House, in the parish of Charlton Musgrove. There was an occupied house here as long ago as 1530. Simon Farewell and his young wife Dorothy, came to live here after their marriage. She was a sister to James Dyer who became Lord Chief Justice of England. The Dyer family lived at nearby Roundhill Grange. The house was still in the Farewell family 200 years later, though much altered. Charles Barton bought the Holbrook Estate in 1846 and greatly enlarged the house, built new stables, erected the lodge and made many other alterations before coming to live here in 1848. John Angerstein purchased the property in 1901 and made more alterations. In 1946 Holbrook House became a country hotel which has just celebrated its half century.

Left: The Pilgrims Rest Public House at Lovington on the road from Castle Cary to Lydford. Once known as the New Inn.

Clanville is a hamlet of the parish of Castle Cary. On the right is Dorset Farm, for many years the home of the Bush family and before them were the Coward's and the Birch's.

North Cadbury Post Office and village shop, also known as Bristol House, which was named after the Bristol/Southampton coach which called here. This has been the village shop and post office since at least 1850. The photograph was taken in 1902 when the building was decorated for the coronation of King Edward VII and Queen Alexandra.

The Mill, West Camel. There had been a mill at West Camel for several centuries until 1928. It was known as the Higher Flour Mill and was part of the Hazelgrove Estate until 1920. The mill building was three stories high, fitted with a complete plant for working two sets of stones, the power being derived from a 12 ft undershoot iron water wheel developing 16 hp. On 27 April 1928 a serious fire destroyed the mill house and the partners in the business, Messrs Ball and Peters ceased trading.

Cucklington Village, c. 1900. The old post office with postman, Sidney Day and his family grouped outside. Next door is the home of shoemaker Henry Pitman. At the time this photograph was taken the properties were already over 150 years old. Part of the Montacute estate were sold in 1895 for the princely sum of seventy pounds.

South Cadbury, c. 1905. South Cadbury Post Office is on the left and was run by Robert Sealey Andrews. The inevitable group of children pose for the camera with (possibly) the nursemaid with baby and pram from the Rectory. Next to the post office is the village school built in 1830. The woman by the garden wall may well be Mrs Cashmore, the village schoolmistress.

Saunders advertisement, 1 December 1933.

Ph. NORTH CADBURY 31.

K. SAUNDERS & Co.,

COAL & COKE MERCHANTS,

Woodside Farm,
SPARKFORD,

Dec: 1ˢᵗ 1933.

M. New: moline

PRICE LIST.

Dear sir

we have pleasure in quoting you
a Special Low Rate for Charity Coal at
North Cadbury.

Good House Coal ∴ 34/6 per ton.

Delivered in Cwts as required.

Thanking you in Anticipation

we remain

yours faithfully

K. Saunders & Co

The Old Ansford Inn at Ansford. In 1740 the sport of cock fighting in this area had its headquarters at the Ansford Inn although the property was much older than that. At one time it was a place of great importance in the area. It was much frequented by the nobility, gentry and travellers in general. The county ball was held here as well as important meetings and auctions. The Tucker family were licencees for many years and Tuckers Lane in the village is named after them. The licence for the inn was surrendered in 1879.

Shepton Montague. This village was known as Scepton in the Domesday Book of 1086 from the Old English for sheep enclosure. The Montague was added some 200 years later from the De Montague family who had come over with William the Conqueror. The parish is made up of several hamlets which are: Higher Shepton, Lower Shepton, Knowle, Stoney Stoke, Welham and South Town.

West Camel, *c.* 1910. A peaceful rural scene, village pond, village green, parish church and a group of cottages. The church of All Saints is fifteenth century but was restored in the nineteenth. The cottages are now one home and, sadly, the pond was filled in some years ago and the site is now the church car park.

Middle Street, Galhampton. Dating from 1935 this scene of Galhampton shows the village shop at Myrtle Cottage which was run by Mrs Annabella Andrews and her son Clarence. On the left is the post office which was run by Miss Flora Hillyer. The village public telephone was here too. Galhampton has had neither shop nor post office for several years now.

Ditcheat Priory was originally attached to the abbey at Glastonbury. Built in the gothic style with a stone roof in 1473 by the then Dean of Wells. The property was moated and had large tithe barns and outbuildings. The carved oak screen in the outer hall records the names and arms of successive rectors since 1433. The house was in fact used as the Rectory for many years.

North Cheriton Post Office. Robert Pickford was sub-postmaster here when this photograph was taken in the 1920s. Fred Hill who was sub-postmaster in the years before the Second World War was also a 'motor car proprietor'. The post office continued here until 1981 when it finally closed. Like so many small villages in the area North Cheriton has no village shop or post office.

Cadbury Castle or Camelot. Trial excavations were held on Cadbury Castle at South Cadbury in June 1913. The excavations took place in the south west corner of the hill said by some to be the 'camelot' of King Arthur. Six men were employed in the excavation work, John Lush of Dorchester, Ernest Vowles of Meare, Dick Hunt, Leonard Edmunds and Henry Caddey of North Cadbury and a Mr Snook of South Cadbury. The levelling rod seen in the lower picture was 10 feet long. Many pieces of pottery of the Romano-British era were found as well as evidence of walls and ramparts and a small child's skeleton. The work was carried out on behalf of the Somerset Archaeological and Natural History Society.

Lower Ansford. These cottages at Lower Ansford belonged to and were occupied by the Dauncey family. The last occupier was Miss Sarah Anna Bettey, daughter of William and Elizabeth (*née* Dauncey) Bettey. Miss Bettey died at 'The Orchards', Ansford where she was living with her nephew Wosson John Barrett. This photograph taken in 1926 shows Sarah Anna and Mary Jane Bettey and two children, Margaret and Elizabeth Barrett.

The Crescent, Compton Pauncefoot, 1911. This crescent of seven three-storey labourers cottages was built by John Husey Hunt in 1820. They were part of the Compton estate until the late 1970s when they were sold, all but one being empty. Seven cottages were then converted to five houses.

Woolston Road, North Cadbury, 1905. Seen outside the post office are the pony and trap that belonged to the Catash Inn. The driver is thought to be Fred Laver, one of the seven sons of 'Shaver' Laver of Rose Cottage. Looking out of her cottage door is Mrs Susannah Morgan (*née* Parker) who died on the first day of the First World War.

Gants Mill at Bruton, but actually in the parish of Pitcombe, *c.* 1940. There is a tradition that weavers from Ghent in Flanders settled here some 300 years ago and it is not too difficult to see how the premises got its name. At one time this was a woollen mill and then a thriving silk trade was carried on here. By the mid-nineteenth century it had become a flour mill and was run by four generations of the Lockyer family from 1858 to 1949. Today it is run as the Mill on the Brue Activity Centre.

Queen Camel. On the left is the village post office which was run by the Gare family for over 120 years. In 1875 the Misses Elizabeth and Tryphena Gare were here, trading as grocers and drapers as well. Later came John Gare who published this view as a postcard. The family were still here in late 1996.

Woolston Road, North Cadbury. This photograph, reproduced from a glass negative, shows the scene in North Cadbury on 25 April 1908 after the severe snowfall which swept the area and caused such consternation. On the left is the end of the beech avenue leading to North Cadbury Court. The trees were already 100 years old, originally twenty-four in number only ten have survived.

Advertisement for Isaac and Perry, January 1935.

Sparkford. New Cottages at Sparkford looking towards the Sparkford Inn which is hidden behind the trees on the left. There is a tradition that in the days when four coaches daily came through the village, two 'up' and two 'down', one coach changed horses at the Sparkford Inn and posting house and it is said that Queen Victoria came through as a baby and during the pause for fresh horses the then innkeeper held her in his arms. Another tradition has it that the last portion of the hangmans rope from Ilchester Gaol was kept at the inn. Squarson Bennett was said to have built or re-built every house in Sparkford except for a few squatters hovels on the road to Camel, which is probably the site of the cottages in this photograph. Carew, King of the Gypsies is said to have died in one of the cottages near to the inn. One cottage at this end of the village was known as 'Maggottybatch' and was home to the village policeman. This strange name may mean a 'plot of land belonging to a woman named Margaret'.

Alhampton. This small village is described as a hamlet of the parish of Ditcheat. This view shows the village shop which closed many years ago and the Alhampton Inn. This part of the village has changed very little over the years.

The New Inn, Galhampton, *c.* 1910. The village inn at Galhampton was opened as a public house in the 1850s and has been open, with the exception for a brief period in the 1980s, ever since. The only real change in the first 100 years was the name which changed to the Harvester and a combine harvester at that. The building on the right was for many years the village smithy and later the garage.

Yarlington House. This view of Yarlington House sometimes known as Yarlington Lodge was taken before 1911 when an extension was added to replace the rather ugly conservatory on the left of the photograph. The house was built in 1785 using materials from the old mansion house in the village. It was built on a rather desolate tree-less area at the top of the village. At the time of building King George III passed along the main road in front of it on his way from Weymouth to Longleat. Seeing the building work in progress the King asked who was doing it. On being informed that it was the work of the new squire who had recently purchased the estate, His Majesty observed 'Ha Ha, a bold man, a bold man indeed to build a house on such a blasted heath'. Yarlington was famous for its great annual fair founded in 1315 which included every kind of entertainment, and is famous for its variety of cider apple, the 'Yarlington Mill' cultivated from a pip found growing at the village mill.

Ditcheat, 1905. This is the village post office run by the Bartlett family and like most village post offices of the time used as the village grocery and drapery store.

North Cadbury Court, c. 1910. This is the south front of the court before extensive alterations were undertaken. The house was built by Sir Francis Hastings in 1581 on the site of an older property. The south front was added in 1799. The north front is Elizabethan and has one window filled with heraldic glass.

Hadspen House in the parish of Pitcombe was built in 1749 by Mr V. Dickersen, incorporating a smaller dwelling. The Hadspen estate was purchased by Henry and Sarah Hobhouse in 1778 and the same family are still in residence today. The Rt Hon Henry Hobhouse became a privy counsellor in 1828 and was keeper of the state papers. He was chairman of Quarter Sessions for the county of Somerset and an active magistrate. Edmund, Bishop Hobhouse and Arthur, Lord Hobhouse were both born here. The grounds of Hadspen House were a favourite venue for Sunday school treats in the late nineteenth and early twentieth centuries. The local dialect name for Hadspen which was Hatchpen was used up until quite recent times.

The Catash Inn, North Cadbury. The Catash takes its name from the Hundred of Catsash (various spellings) of which North Cadbury was part. It was built in 1796 and was a 'peoples refreshment house association' house between the wars. The Cat as it is sometimes familiarly known has been a public house for a full two hundred years and used to be known as the Cadbury Inn.

Stavordale Priory is in the parish of Charlton Musgrove and was formerly a priory of canons of the Augustinian Order. It was founded in the thirteenth century by the Lovell family but much of what remains is fifteenth century. In 1904 the property was carefully restored to some of its former glory after some of the buildings had been used to house farm animals.

The Mill, Queen Camel, 1910. Mentioned in the Domesday Book and obviously re-built several times over the centuries, this mill continued in use until 1940 when a fire destroyed the building. The mill was powered by a water wheel which was driven by water controlled by hatches. These hatches are preserved as a feature within the modern house built on the site and water still flows through them. George Kiddle was the miller here in 1875, the Rood brothers during and after the First World War and Messrs Evans and Morland at the time of the fire.

Compton Castle, 1904. This house was built in 1820 by John Husey Hunt. It is in a beautiful setting of wooded hills with a large lake and feeder streams. The whole Compton estate was offered for sale in 1911 and was purchased by Sir William Mason (later Lord Blackford). Compton Castle later came into the possession of the Showering family of Shepton Mallet.

Redlynch House, 1905. Redlynch came into the possession of Sir Stephen Fox in 1670. Sir Stephen was a great favourite of King Charles II and lived in the reigns of six sovereigns. He was described as 'the greatest favourite of princes, the chiefest minister of state and the wealthiest subject in the realm'. He was the projector of Chelsea Hospital to which he contributed large sums of money. He rebuilt the mansion at Redlynch in 1672 on the site of the old chapel. His son, Stephen was created Lord Ilchester and Stavordale and Baron of Redlynch in 1746 and Earl of Ilchester in 1756. He also enjoyed the favour of princes and was a favourite of King George III who often stayed at Redlynch. The property was by all accounts two houses connected by a covered passage. This passage was removed early in the nineteenth century and the houses were known as the East and West Mansions. In 1913 the East Mansion was demolished and in 1914 the west part which was undergoing alterations was burnt down by suffragettes. It was then re-built the following year.

Compton Road, South Cadbury. Reproduced from a glass negative taken in 1910. In the centre is the Red Lion public house, which was previously known as the New Inn. At the time the photographer visited South Cadbury, Charles Chamberlain was the landlord. Note the tap in the wall to the right of the woman peeping from her doorway.

The Parish Church of St Mary, Yarlington and the last portion of the old Berkeley Manor House. This house was home to several owners of the Yarlington estate until 1782 when it was abandoned in favour of the new house on the Sherborne/Bruton road. The house then gradually fell into decay and the final parts were demolished in the 1950s.

Galhampton Manor looks much the same today as it did when this photograph was taken in the 1920s. It was built in the late seventeenth century but has twentieth-century additions. The property belonged to the Melliar family of Wells and was let to a succession of tenants in the eighteenth and nineteenth centuries.

The Main Street in Qqueen Camel. On the left is the Supply Stores built about 1901 and still trading under the same name today. Note the delightfully posed groups of children and adults and the carriage, the only traffic. Queen Camel is still a very desirable village marred only by a constant stream of traffic.

Yarlington village can boast of some unusual house names: Pin Lane Cottage, Sticklepark Cottages, Fishermans Hut, Snail Farm and Crows Nest. The lady occupier of the last named was once reported to the authorities for running an 'ale house' without a licence. The first three names survive, the fourth has been renamed and Crows Nest was demolished many years ago. The same fate also befell the group of thatched cottages furthest from the camera. The other thatched cottage has recently undergone a very thorough modernisation and has lost its thatch in favour of tiles.

Church Road, Sparkford, early in the twentieth century. Kynastons shop is on the right, where a Dames School once stood. Pamela Kynaston ran her little shop with her niece, Lavinia. Miss Pamela could neither read nor write but if asked could put her finger on the correct entry of debt in her ledgers. On sundays Pamela wore a brilliant blue dress to church and Lavinia an equally brilliant purple one. Opposite this cottage was an orchard in which was a derelict and some said haunted cottage. An unusual place name beyond the church at Sparkford was known as Lickhill Knapp. The name 'lick' may have the same derivation as 'lych' for a ghostly funeral procession was often seen to make its way to the church.

The Blackmore Vale hunt at the New Inn at Galhampton, c. 1912. They would appear to have stopped for refreshments, a scene that could not happen today, as it would cause traffic congestion and an accident or two.

WEST CAMEL.

West Camel, 1906. On the right is the village school established in 1818. It became a National School in 1837 and the County Education Authority took over in 1903. It closed in 1948. The parochial church council then purchased the building for use as a church hall. To the left of the school the rectory can be seen which had been built on the site of the old Grange belonging to the Abbots of Muchelney. A 'modern' extension to the house was added in the 1820s. In the grounds is a circular dovecote.

WOSSON BARRETT & Cº,

Wholesale & Family Grocers,

HOME & COLONIAL PRODUCE MERCHANTS,

BACON & HAM CURERS. PORK BUTCHERS & SAUSAGE MAKERS,

SEEDSMEN, FRUITERERS AND TOBACCONISTS,

MINERAL WATERS. PATENT MEDICINES. **CASTLE CARY.**

FAMILIES OWN BACON & HAMS CAREFULLY SMOKED.
AGENTS FOR ROGERS' A.K. ALES & STOUT IN BOTTLES & CASKS.

VIEW OF INTERIOR.

Wosson Barrett Advertisement.

Three

School Days

Sunny Hill School, Bruton, c. 1910. Sunny Hill was founded in October 1900 as a public secondary school for girls. It was formerly opened by the Marquis of Bath. A new wing was added in 1912 and further additions made in 1937. It is now known as the Bruton School for Girls.

Above: Sexeys football fixtures, 1937 to 1938.

Left: North Cheriton SchooL. The headmaster, Mr David Gibson with his last eleven pupils in May 1977. The school closed for good on 21 July 1977. The children are: David Bennett, Roger Winters, Darren Higgins, Clare Layden, Gregory Foot, Douglas Dores, Shaun Higgins, Helen Winters, Desmond Layden, Heide Dores and Carren James.

The staff of Ansford Secondary Modern School, July 1948. Back row, left to right: Mrs N. Stokes, Mr J. Harrison, Mrs J. Harrison, Mr R. Collett, Mr Davis, Mr H. Reed, Miss D. Haynes, Mr K. Smith, Mr E. Brown. Front row, left to right: Miss B. Francis, Miss T. Phillips, Mr H. Gough, the headmaster, Miss Wickenden, Miss V. Brown.

Castle Cary Public Elementary School. This school was built in 1840 and enlarged in 1876 to accommodate 380 children. In the last year it has been enlarged and modernized again and is now known as Castle Cary County Primary School.

Tuckers babes, 1961. The first group at Ansford to take the G.C.E. examination. A small group split off in the fourth year and were the first to stay until they were 16. Back row, left to right: Graham Heath-Coleman, Roberta Ball, Mary March, Angela Moore, Jean Keirl. Front row, left to right: Sheila Crawford, Julie Lawrence, Ruth White, Beryl Mundy and Norman Sansom.

Sunny Hill School at Bruton. This is one of a set of six postcards of the school and dates from the 1920s. Note the girls rolling the tennis court.

Sexeys school group, 1924. Back row, left to right: Dudley Hansford, -?-, Thomas Dolman, Malcolm Edwards, Bernard James. Next row, left to right: William Heath, Leonard Jobbins, Charles Baker (the form comedian), John Sanders, Alan Gare, James Bryant, Charles Pither, Alan Hamblin. Next row, left to right: Eric Marsh, Eric Cole, Arthur Joynt, ? Dawes, W.A. Knight (the headmaster), D.J. Williams (english and history teacher) E.H. White, Frank Talbot, Rodney Scammell. Front row, left to right: Francis Griffiths (a good footballer), Bernard Murley, Fred Hunt (died in 1928 of T.B.), John Hutchings, Ronald Symes, Douglas Crofts, Hubert Laver.

North Cheriton School, 1971. Back row, left to right: David Gibson (the headmaster), Peter Judd, Stuart Nicholls, Andrew Gibson, Mark Crofts, Stephen Adams, Nigel Masters, Paul Entwistle, Peter Sims, Edward Dyke, Mrs Goddard (the only other teacher). Second row, left to right: John Wetherall, John Dicker, Nigel Vaughan, Ben Sherry, Timothy Judd, Joann Wetherall, Gail Dyke, Martyn Gibson, Mark Sims, Richard Reed, William Rawlings, Paul Bennett, Mark Day. Third row, left to right: Bridget Wetherall, Nicola Masters, Lucy Allen, Helen Allen, Alison Hockey, Edwin Dicker, Judy Bentley, Diana Nicholls, Elizabeth Hockey, Karen Reed, Cherry Woods. Front row, left to right: Allan Dicker, Paul Adams, David Day, Alan Rawlings, Philip Rawlings, Andrew Allen, Richard Garner, David Bennett.

Miss Grosvenors School, Castle Cary, late 1920s. The girls include: Joan Harrison, Vere Churchouse, Brenda Snook, Olive Parsons, Frances Phillips, Marjorie Gifford, Gwen Phillips, Dorothy Green, Grace Shepherd, Una Phillips, Betty Wride, Mary Snook. The boys are: Claude Clothier, Donald Pither, Peter Pitman, Les Phillips, Harry Snook, Guy Churchouse, Cyril Clothier and Conrad Snook.

North Cadbury School Group, 1923. Back row, left to right: -?-, Clarence Andrews, Jack Jones, Fred McGarry, Pat McGarry, -?-, Ernest Foote. Next row, left to right: Phyllis Randall, Ivy Randall, Molly McGarry, Kathleen Oborn, -?-, Kitty Laver, -?-, Gladys Clothier. Front row, left to right: -?-, Les Wilton, Philip Pitman, May Caddey, Mr Smye (class teacher), Vera Thomas, -?-, Jack Rimen.

Castle Cary school, the infants, 1916. Top row, left to right: Arthur Upham, Eddie Lockyer, Reg Whereat, Stanley Bird, Victor Strickland, Bert Targett, Albert Lockett, Fred Hurst, Eddy Vaux. Second row, left to right: Ted Chamberlain, Frank Fussell, Percy Parsons, Harold White, Jimmy Keys, Doug Pound, Leonard (Pat) Hall, Harry Lees, Walter Parsons. Third row, left to right: Jack Otton, Winnie Brown, Margaret Meaden, Kate Peatty, Doris Hill, Beatie Weeks, -?-, Beatie Pearce, Dorcas Veryard, Phyllis White. Front row, left to right Edna Ware, -?-, Effie Cooper, Gertie Eaton, Doris Callan, -?-, ? Hedditch, Kitty Parsons, Zena Ings.

Kings School, Bruton. King Edward the VI Grammar School at Plox, Bruton was founded in 1519 by Richard Fitzjames, Bishop of London, Sir John Fitzjames, his nephew and in 1526 Lord Chief Justice of England and John Edmondes. The school was supressed at the Reformation and restored by King Edward in 1549. Hugh Sexey was a governor of the school from 1599 to 1619. R.D. Blackmore, the author of *Lorna Doone* was a pupil here. New school buildings were erected in 1920 as a memorial to those members of the school who had fallen in the First World War of 1914 to 1918.

Compton Pauncefoot School and schoolhouse were built in 1858 for 80 children from the villages of Compton Pauncefoot and Blackford. It remained open for just over 100 years.

Castle Cary School Group, 1952. Back row, left to right: Alan Harrison, Barry Caddey, Terry Higdon, Raymond Painter, Ian Cliff, Michael Chivers, Michael Mears, Peter Wyatt. Middle row, left to right: Ann Rowswell, Colin Webber, Roger Otton, Derek Talbott, Derek Biles, Gordon Stockman, John Hayward, John Chilcott, Christopher Squibb, Michael Clothier, Michael Donisthorpe, Mary Handsford. Front row, left to right: Christine Laver, Vera Adams, Helen Smith, Wendy Cook, Mary Collet, Anthea Haskins, Hazel Cave, June Baker, Hazel Bloomfield, -?-.

North Cadbury School Group, c. 1918. Miss Kathleen Ryall is the teacher and some of the children are: Vera Brain, Milly Laver, Maggie Hunt, Joan Sebright, Dick Morrish, Albert Hyde, Lawrence Rowe and Harold Baker. Miss Ryall was a pupil here herself, then a monitor, pupil teacher and teacher.

Sexeys school at Bruton was founded in November 1889 out of the endowments of Sexeys Hospital and opened on 6 April 1891 in temporary premises at the Glen, Bruton. On the first day 15 boys arrived for lessons. The formal opening took place on 19 April 1892 with 57 boys on the register. The site of the new buildings was known as 'Solomons Cliffs'.

North Cheriton School was built in 1846 to accommodate 80 children from North Cheriton and Holton parishes. This group was photographed in 1968. Back row, left to right: Mrs Goddard, John Wetherall, Nigel Masters, Mark Crofts, Andrew Fudge, Ian Gibson, Andrew Gibson, Peter Judd, Paul Entwistle, David Gibson (the headmaster), Mark Day. Second row, left to right: Edward Dyke, Suzanne Dyke, Judy Masters, Sally Wetherall, Angela Fudge, Rosemary Smith, Josephine Judd, Susan Keady, Ruth Lazenbury, Doreen Marshall, Martyn Gibson. Third row, left to right: Lucy Allen, Bridget Wetherall, Jackie Barrington, Joann Wetherall, Lynn Davis, Carol Burman, Gail Dyke, Nicola Masters, Helen Allen. Front row, left to right: John Dicks, Mark Sims, Peter Sims, Ben Sherry, Edwin Dicker, Paul Bennett.

Queen Camel School, 1904. The school at Queen Camel was built in 1872 at the sole expense of Hervey St John Mildmay for 120 children. It was given to Queen Camel by Mr St John Mildmay as a memorial to his parents and is known as the Countess Gytha County Primary School. Village dances were held in the schoolroom before the village hall was built. The old village school was directly opposite the new and was demolished about the same time as the new one was built. In the background is the old mill.

North Cadbury Village School and adjoining school house was built in 1875 to accommodate 140 children from the parish (North Cadbury, Galhampton and Woolston). The school logbook of 7 March 1906 says that 'the children were photographed after school this afternoon'. This is the photograph and although no pupil has been identified we can be sure that some, with names such as Laver, Hunt, Clothier, Chamberlain, Kempster, Pitman, Jennings, Collins and Herman are represented.

Staff v School netball match at Ansford School, April 1950. The school team was: B. Garland, J. Skipper, A. Reynolds, R. Hendes, B. Meaden, E. Wingrove, V. Perrrot. The staff were: Miss M. Passingham, Miss M. Stark, Mrs M. Harrison, Miss V. Brown, Miss B. Francis, Miss J. Lush (O.S.), Miss I. Day. The final score was 11 – 9 in the staff's favour.

Compton Pauncefoot School Maypole Dancers, c. 1928. This photograph is thought to have been taken in the grounds of Compton Rectory. The teacher, on the extreme right is Miss Gwen Stewart but none of the children has been identified. If you look closely at the third boy from the right you can see that he moved as the photographer took the picture with the result that he appears to have three legs! Miss Stewart was soon to move to North Cadbury school as the infants mistress, where she would stay for 45 years. She became one of the most respected teachers in the area.

Queen Camel School. Senior pupils and teachers on a visit to the *Evening World* newspaper offices in Bristol, in 1932. Front row, left to right: Wyndham Hewlett, Geoffrey Biggin, Herbert A'Court, Kenneth Martin, James Toop, Arthur Roberts, George Short, William Hallett, Walter Windsor. Second row, left to right: Henry Ralph, William Shire, Lawrence Brooks, Harold Elkins, Bernard Hoddinott, Mary Anderson, Phyllis Spencer, Alice Bond, Albert Williams, Ruby Partridge, Eileen Falloon. Back row, left to right: William Miller, Mr Wheeler (deputy headmaster), Greville March, John Lambert, Maurice Chainey, Wyndham Hurford, Harold Watts, Winifred Biggs, Lawrence Martin, Isobel Lambert, Norman Toop, Ruby Hatcher, Mr John Lane (headmaster), Frank Whittle, Muriel Coleman, Doris Hutchings, Albert Perry, Geoffrey Brooks, William Higgins, Dorothy Giles, Alice Commins and Miss Harrill.

North Cadbury School Group, *c.* 1927. The staff are the headmaster, Mr Avery and his assistant Miss Effie Goodfellow (later to become Mrs Ted Barrington). The pupils include: Nancy Marsh, Joyce Hunt, Doris Parker, Dorothy Catton, Richard Avery, Gerry Toms, Peter Sebright and Jack Dyer.

Compton Pauncefoot Group. Possibly the last children at this school before it was closed in 1960/61. Back row, left to right: Godfrey Miles, Adrian Fry, Richard Mead, David Biddiscombe, Danny Fry, -?-, Morley Snook, -?-, -?-, Colin Miles and Tim Turner. Front row, left to right: -?- , -?-, -?-, Julie Elliott, Caroline Rendall, Jane Miles, Carol Coleman, Richard Elliott, ? Potter. The children are photographed with the headmistress, Miss Bicknell and the dinner lady, Mrs Dewberry.

Ansford School group, 1948. Back row, left to right: Betsy Trott, Grace Parsons, Donald Sibley, Harold Smith?, Betty Osborne, Vera Brown, Gordon Marshall, Ethel Guppy, Morley Spencer, ? Charles, Doris Wiltshire, Audrey Lambert. Middle row, left to right: Evelyn Davis, Graham Wreford, Pam Jefferies, Tony Fowler, Dennis Thorner, -?-, Dave Newport. Front row, left to right: Josie Howard, David Hart, Ann Higgins, -?-, -?- and Pat Martin?

Four

Pastimes

Charabanc Trip from North Cadbury, c. 1925. This all male group from North Cadbury visiting Gough's Caves at Cheddar includes: James Berry (the sexton), John Rowe (the baker), William Randall (the carpenter), Cyril Foote (the builder), Dick Hunt (the publican), Jim Clothier (the mason), Dick King (the gravedigger), Sam Paynter (the watch and clockmaker), Fred Raymond, Walter Hunt, Percy and Fred Foote, Edward Hunt and Charlie Ryall.

East Somerset Skittles Dinner. Those identified in North Cadbury Village Hall include: Bert Bond, Hubert Snook, Walt Hunt, Nat Higgins, Bert Bishop, Harold Miles, Alfie Bilbrough, Ken Davis, Alf Priest, Cecil McCann, Jack Bartlett, Lionel Laver, Jack Bartlett (2), Sam and Verd Wake, Len Winslade, Jack Noonan, Harold Stone, Jack Caddey, George Martin, Jack Foote, Ron Fear, George Foot, Harry Clothier, Ken King, Geoff Newman, Jack Otton, Bill and Harold Sherrell, Cyril Clothier, Bill Bartlett, Ted Rays, Eric Sheppard, Fred Hodges, Bert Southway, ? Whitehead, ? King.

Skittles presentation night at the Red Lion, South Cadbury in 1959. Left to right: Nat Higgins, Arthur Wivell, Sam Wake, Norman Rendell, Mike Skipper, Charlie Best, Verd Wake, Gordon Rendell, Allan Bartlett, Fred Newport and George Frapple.

Dance to the Lukins Band at North Cadbury Village Hall. Those present include: Eileen Clothier, Maureen and Brian Herman, Kathy Miller, Betty and Vera Brain, Norman and Gladys Lloyd Jones, Horace Matthews, Thomas Pyke, Ruth Lush, Teresa Arnold?, Jack Talbot?, John Dill, Beryl Meaden, Dave Hart, Brian Pitman, Neil Edworthy, Daphne Yeabsley, John Pitman, Clive Chambers, Richard Phillips, Norman White, Dave Lush, Margaret Brine.

Wincanton Summer Carnival, 1965. The summer carnival was an annual event at Wincanton for some 30 years from the end of the Second World War. Pictured here is the carnival queen, Miss J. Hartnell. The Hartnell family had a bakers shop in South Street, Wincanton until quite recently.

Coronation Day Group at Charlton Musgrove, 1911. This postcard was sent to Monty Morrish at North Cadbury by John Dyke (they were related by marriage) of Charlton Musgrove and presumably he is in the group which appears to be entirely male.

Wedding group at Yarlington, 1924. The wedding was between Lottie Masters and Bernard House who are sitting behind their bridesmaids. The clergyman stood in the doorway was the Rector of Yarlington, Revd Boyd. Sat on the extreme left is Miss Crees and third in the same row is Samuel Brooks Bartlett. Other families represented in this picture are Ashford, Darknell and Wyatt.

Outing from North Cadbury, 1933. The bellringers and their families from the parish church at North Cadbury. Standing, left to right: Mr and Mrs Jack Alway, -?-, Revd Moline, James and Trevor Kempster, Elsie, Jim and Phyllis Laver, Len Davis, Bill Parker. Kneeling: Walter Tyley and an unidentified woman. Sitting, left to right: Sam and Eliza Laver, -?-, Walter Parker, -?-, Walter and Freda Laver, -?-.

Womens Institute fete at North Cadbury, c. 1948. Included here are Doris and Roy King, Mary Chambers, Sylvia Sebright, Bessie Cox, Joan and Bill Raymond, Mrs Munday and Mrs Ryall, Gwen Stewart, Kathleen, Roger and Cecelia Cock, Phyllis and Shirley Laver, Irene and Sally Newport, Pauline Winslade, Alan Bartlett, Nora, Tim and Ann Miller and Virginia Porter.

Old Comrades Carnival at Castle Cary, 1922. Ex-servicemen and their families parade from South Cary to Maggs' Lane for a fete held in a field (now the site of Ansford School), on August Bank Holiday Monday. The girl on the bicycle is Kathleen Pike of Galhampton with her mother stood next to her. Bill Derrett is on the horse and Jack Weeks on the pony.

Children of Ansford on Jubilee Day, 6 May 1935, in the Horse Show field. Left to right: Valerie Fletcher, Eileen Francis, Brenda Francis, Stella Groves, Sheila Groves, Vera Bleak, Sarah Barrett, Jean Lanning, Ron Hicks, Veronica Sewell, Sylvia Stockman.

Right: Coronation Day at Bruton, 1937. The days proceedings commenced with a special celebration of the Holy Eucharist, conducted by the Revd R.T.S. Tolson of Ansford. At West End a procession was formed, which proceeded to the parish church for a united service. It was headed by Bruton Town Band under bandmaster, Mr G. Steeds with Mr A. England as chief standard-bearer. Represented were the Parish Council, British Legion, West Wilts Society, Girl Guides, Junior Athletics Club, Womens Institute, Red Cross, Foresters Court, Cubs and Boy Scouts, Brownies. In this picture the procession has reached the premises of Thomas' drapers and shoe shop in the High Street.

Below: North Cadbury Cricket Club, early 1930s. Standing, left to right: -?-, Reg Sebright Fred Windsor, Len Davis, Bill Jones, -?-, Reg Hunt and in front are Ran Raymond, ? Merchant, Fred Simons, ? Merchant, W.H. (Roger) Laver.

North Cadbury United Friendly Society, 1900. At Parsonage Farm (now Rowlands) North Cadbury. Back row, left to right: Dick King, -?-, Mr Parker, -?-, Silas Laver, -?-, -?-, -?-, Mr Parker, Thomas Fox, -?-, -?-, Jack Chamberlain, -?-, -?-, -?-, a groom at Rowlands, William Lang (the village policeman), a groom at Rowlands. Middle row, left to right: William 'Shaver' Laver, -?-, Sam Hunt, Frank Hunt, Jim Hunt, Alfred Hunt, Jacob Holt, -?-, Joe West, a groom at Rowlands. Front row, left to right: Bert Hunt (the last survivor), -?-, James Foote -?-, -?-, Esau Bennett, Bill Hunt, Mechab Mead, Sam Foote, Harry Pitman, Ernest Hunt and four men from Compton Pauncefoot.

North Cheriton, Maperton and Holton members of the Home Guard. Back row, left and right: C. Snook, R. Lloyd, L. McCreadie, Dr Edwards, R. McCreadie, H. Avery, ? House, A. Polden, V. Watts, W. Martin. Middle Row: W. Martin, W. Banting, ? Baker, Sir Digby Lawson, C. Dunford, W. Newman, W. Paull, ? Collins. Front Row, left to right: B. Butler, ? Hughes, A. Cole, J. Rowden, -?-.

Wincanton Cork Club. This club was based at the George in Mill Street, Wincanton during the early years of the twentieth century. A member of this club was obliged to carry a cork with him at all times. If challenged by another member and unable to produce his cork he had to pay a fine which was kept in a box by the landlord. The box was emptied once a year and paid for a charabanc trip. Here the members can be seen after one of their outings. Some are wearing buttonholes and what a variety of hats!

At Squibbs Garage, Castle Cary. Left to right: Mont Squibb, Cecil Powell, Harry Cooper, Frank Lanning, Harry Powell, William Fletcher, Gilbert Fletcher, Bert Barber, George Squibb (the boss), Bill Stride and Jim Squibb stand in front of a Ford Sedan old model T. The dog belonged to a master at Sexey's School. 'When he went to the First World War, Squibbs had the dog. They took him back when he came back. They took him back Saturday afternoon but he was back again Sunday morning. They took him back 2 or 3 times and in the end he said you had better keep him'.

Lady skittlers from North Cadbury. Left to right: Margaret Hamer, Kate McKee, Evelyn White, May Davis, Bessie Sherring, Vera Brain, Monica Lamb, Helen Attwell and Ada McCann.

North Cadbury P.T.A., Playford Dances, 1976. Left to right: Lesley Hornsby, -?-, John Pearse, Joyce Hale, Geoffrey Barnes, Vanda Coulsey, Martin Coulsey, Eileen White, Ron Cameron, Jean Cameron, Fred Ryley, Rosalie Ryley. In front, left to right: Jane Pearse, Gordon Hale, Kay Attwell, Jim Lukins, Marion Lukins and Alan White.

Bruton, 1937. The committee elected to organise the arrangements for celebrating the coronation of King George VI and Queen Elizabeth. Left to right: C.E. Grocott, A.E. Butt (the secretary), Mrs Peacocke, J. Steeds, H. Satow (the chairman), W.J. Clothier, Mrs E. Jones, J. Chancellor, G. Hobbs and E. Knoylls.

Sparkford Market. A large gathering on market day in 1925, which included Edward Cornish of Manor Farm, Galhampton. Most heads turn to the camera, even the cows and everyone wore a hat.

The Mothers' Union in the Castle Cary Deanery present *Called to Witness* in eighteen tableaux at North Cadbury Village Hall on 17 April 1951. Those taking part were the Mothers' Union branches of Ansford, Castle Cary, Cucklington, Evercreech, Keinton Mandeville, Maperton, North Cadbury and Wincanton. Also the Women's Guild of South Cadbury and Sutton Montis and the North Cadbury branch of CEMS. Here the North Cadbury members take their turn on stage. Included are: Mesdames Winslade, Warren, Laver, Stewart, Clothier, Amor and Miss Shirley Laver.

West Camel Church Choir, 1960. Back row, left to right: Nicola Lawrence, Heather White, Les Dawson, Norman Sansom, Roger Dawson, Harold Lawrence, Ron Sansom. Middle row, left to right: Angela White, Amanda Lawrence, Nicholas Case, Richard White, Felicity Goodman, Annette Wilson, Revd Ralph-Bowman, Susan Kennett, Heather Barker, Robert Whitemore, Andrew Case, Christopher Wreford, Paul Sweby, Jane Goodman, Granville Barker. In front are: Richard Whitemore and Robert Pemberton.

Wincanton carnival, 1922. Third from the left at the back, with the 'stars and moons' is
Kathleen Downton. On the front left is Ellen Downton, next to her is Florence Stone and fifth
from the left is her sister Beatrice Stone. The Downton sisters lived at Bayford and the Stone
sisters at Penselwood. From the message on the rear of the photograph we know that Ellen went
as 'summer' and it seems likely that Kathleen went as 'night'. The girl on the right looks like
'winter' and the man on the right could be 'the grim reaper'. The woman in the centre would
appear to have the 'horn of plenty'.

Skittlers from the Harvester, Galhampton. Back row, left to right: Owen Cox, Leslie Bartlett,
Lew Hamer, Jim Holland, Mike Herman, Maurice Herman, Harry Bartlett, Gordon Sansom,
Des Sexton. Sitting, left to right: -?-, Ken King, Walter Hunt and Brian Herman. In front are Tim
Stretton, Len Hooper and Harold Herman.

Queen Camel Air Cadets, 1955. Back row, left to right: Charlie Clothier, Pete Kitchener, David Pengelly, Terry Higgins, Bobby Greenway, Dave Abbott and four unknown. Front row, left to right: Ian Gare, Barry Fowler, David Jenkins, Johnnie Doel, Brian Guest, Keith Pardoe, Pete Roberts.

Ansford Church Choir and Sunday School, c. 1953. Back row, left to right: Roy Shiner, Mrs Walter Hallett, Miss Warren, Henry Church, Eileen Carpenter, Betty Hole, Brenda Francis, Stella Groves, Penny Pitman, Hazel Heathman, Ernie Chivers, John Pitman, Richard Pitman, Bob Hedditch, Brian Pitman. Second row, left to right: Brian Sharley, Les Burbidge, Rene Carpenter and Wendy Cook. Sitting, left to right: Barbara Cave, Eileen Cave, Rosemary Carpenter, Robin Wines, Terry Sharley, John Carpenter, Josie Chivers, Michael Chivers, Dulcie Hedditch, -?-.

The Jolly Waggoners performed *Latter Lammas*, a dialect play by John Read at Castle Cary Town Hall in 1938. This was the first time the play had been performed in its entirety although scenes from it were presented in 1911 by the 'Old Sexeians' Amateur Dramatic Society. *Latter Lammas* takes its title from an old Somerset term of reproach applied to a person who was slow, unpunctual or lacked diligence. The play depicted life in a Somerset village in the 1830s. The Jolly Waggoners were connected with the Congregational church at Castle Cary. Shown here are, back row, left to right: William Heath, Leslie Corp, Hugh Thomas, David Gass, Gwen Green, Neville Newport, Archie Cooper, Percy Hill, John Fry. Front row, left to right: Joyce Pullen, Evelyn Radford, Molly Chamberlain, Mary Cooper, Norman Hutchfield, Dennis Phillips, John Bulley, Ruth Bennett, Phyllis Cave, Rene Pullen, Nancy Le Tisier, Margaret Milligan. The play was produced by D.J. Glass.

Castle Cary Chamber of Commerce, 1974. Back row, left to right: Fred Chancellor, Chris Squibb, Richard Drewett, Clive Walters, Graham Walters. Second row, left to right: Mark Jones, Frank Parker, Jack Otton, Hubert Laver. Third row, left to right: Tom Trowbridge, Ken Youings, Graham Clothier, Robin Young, Graham Asher, Arthur Thorne, Ted Lush, Ron Hicks. Front row, left to right: Beryl Chancellor, Bid Otton, Sam Phillips, Stella Clothier, Olive Laver, Joan Sansom, Kathleen Thorne and Vera Walters.

Pantomime at North Cadbury, 1969. *Cinderella* written by Pam McIver was performed by Jane Penny, Clair and Lesley Harris, Naomi Lawson, Jessie Davis, Philip Felstead, Russell Kinsey, Sue Cadmore, David and Michael Sparkes, Christine Wyatt, Tim Franklin, Jill and Helen Bowcock, Amanda, Kirsty and David McIver, Heather and Katrina Raison, Perrin and Philippa Felstead, Victoria Elks, Vanda Coulsey, Sally Parsons, Jill and Janet Northover, Helen, Debbie, Matthew and Mark Bentham, Frances de Salis and Catherine Sparkes.

The staff of Thomas', Castle Cary on their annual outing to Tintern Abbey. Back row, left to right: Harry Wilton, Bill Thomas, Ron Dunford, Bill Harris, Wilf Chance, Fred Weeks, Hugh Thomas, John Thomas, Harry Rapson, Ted White, Sam Veryard, Harry Creed and Jim Cox. Front row, left to right: Jack Caddey, Harry Mills, Charlie Harris, Henry Milborne, Charlie Perrott, Fred Mills?, Percy Thomas, Frank Sermon, George Weeks, Fred Sweetman, Ben Paul and Sid Harris.

A visit to Robinsons of Avonmouth by local farmers arranged by George Martin of Galhampton on 1 October 1937. Sitting for the photographer are: Edward Cornish, William Osborn, Mr and Mrs A. Pitman, Miss J. Pitman, Ernest Anthony, Edgar Bartlett, William Heath, George Martin, Robert Stewart, Berkeley Watts, Leslie Bartlett?, Tom Pitman and some unidentified.

A Shakespearian play performed in Castle Cary Town Hall in 1925 and produced by Miss Woodforde. Includes: Mabel Woodforde, Muriel Taylor, May Fox, Kath Newport, Win Laver, Isabel Weeks, Laura Stride, May Davis, Peggy Dodd and Marie Hill.

Castle Cary Bible Class. The Bible class was started in Castle Cary in 1918 in a bid to help the young lads of the town. At one time there were up to 70 present. The classes started in the carpet room at Pithers Emporium before moving to the Congregational church. At one time the class would go to the top of Lodge Hill and sing popular hymns that could be heard all over the town. Here class members meet on the cricket field. Back row, left to right: Arthur Bellamy, Reg Parsons, Ernie Francis, Walter Parsons, Percy Roper, Basil Troake, Harold White, Charlie Targett, George Russell, Denis Pither. Fourth row: Ted Chamberlain, Percy Parsons, -?-, Percy Hunt, Lewis Martin, Bert Targett, Jack Giles, Fred Tuck, Bob Pitman, Bert Vallis, Alex Sweet. Third row, left to right: David Gass, Roy Pither, Jimmy Keys Junior, Keith Davis, -?-, Billy Waterman, Ernie Ridout, Ronald Simms, Jack Mogg, Willie Tuck, Jack Creed, -?-, Jimmy Keys Senior. Second row, left to right: Bob Eaton, Edgar Warr, Fred Weeks, Frank Ridout, Reg White, Roy Loader, John Pither, Jack Weeks, Claude Newport, Herbie Meaden, Lewis Dossaer, Bert Cox. Front row, left to right: Donald Pither, -?-, Ernie Stockman, Wilf Laver, Walter Chamberlain, Bert Pitman, Terence Brake, Bill Peaty.

Castle Cary Cycle Club was revived in 1905. They are seen here at South Cary on Sunday 5 October 1930. Left to right: V.E. Strickland (sub-captain), C. Kirkby, Peter Pitman, -?-, B. Cox, K. Baker, F. Ridout, W. James, J. Cox (the club mascot aged 13), L. Dossaer, ? Badger, J.T. Pike (captain), S. Stockman, R. Keys, W.T. Poole (chairman), H.W. Pitman (treasurer), E. Chamberlain, L. Webb, W. Chamberlain, R. Pitman, P. Vallis, J. Loader, A. Parsons, A. Penny.

Castle Cary Football Club, season 1922-1923. Back row, left to right: Tom Biss, Bill Chamberlain, Frank Parker, W. Perry, Billy Francis, Claude Phillips, Arthur Wade, Jack Chamberlain, Ted Asher, Joe Tullett. Second row, left to right: Walter Vallis, Bill 'Sheppey' Davis (the fastest thing on two legs), Doug Sims, Freddie Wines, Sam Perrott (the hardest head in Cary) and in front are F. Martin and Brian Bees.

In Merricks Yard at the rear of the triangle at Castle Cary, when Billy Poole had his cycle shop at the bottom of the yard, 1920s. Left to right, Dolly Veryard, Fanny Garland, Hilda Poole, Jim Garland, Billie Poole, Herbert Quick, Mrs Poole, George Bolson, S.J. Phillips, Lily Poole. Prior to his cycle business Mr Poole had a ginger beer bottling plant in the same premises.

Ansford Sunday School picking primroses to decorate the church for Easter Sunday, early 1930s. Afterwards they would be given tea at Wyke courtesy of Mr and Mrs Phillips. Included here are: Ernie Chivers, Bert Lodge, Mary, Betty and Anita Whittle, Sheila and Stella Groves, Ron and Stan Hicks, Marian and Ken Clothier, Ted Ranger, Bill Stockman, Jack James and Ignatius the dog.

Castle Cary church choir and churchwardens, 1951. Back row, left to right: Stuart Kemp, John Stokes, Arthur Martin. Second row, left to right: Charlie Chilcott, Percy Curtis, Sidney Hearn, Herbert Newport, Revd Kemp, Ernie Meaden, Harry Collings, Ernie Ridout, Bill Stride. Third row, left to right: Michael Donisthorpe, Terry Higdon, Geoff Ruddle, Les Stokes, John Chilcott, Tony Higdon, Derek Talbot. Fourth row, left to right: Hilda Poole, Mrs Cooper, Derek Biles, Robert Strickland, David Warr, Tony Perrott, Ian Cliff, Iris Porter, Dollie Curtis. Front row, left to right: Pete Strickland, Roger Otton and John Hayward.

Mr and Mrs Tullett's staff annual summer outing. They are seen here in 1926 on the lawn at Cheddar after a strawberry tea. In the winter they would be taken to a pantomime. Back row, left to right: Fred Neck, Dennis Meaden, May Swattridge, Edie Troakes*, Tom Trowbridge. Middle row, left to right: Nellie Meaden, Ivy Pitman, Joe Tullett, Christine Tullett, Mrs Tullett, Maude Cooper* and Christine's nanny. Front row, left to right: Alice Green*, Fred Tuck and Connie Cotton. Those marked with a * worked in Mrs Tullett's dressmaking shop in Woodcock Street.

Castle Cary Flower Show, 1951. Left to right: Bill May, Geoff Laver, Hubert Laver, Grace Yeabsley, Winnie Pike, John Bulley, Jack Pike, George Yeabsley, Len Joslin, Ernie Hunt, Olive Thomas, Percy Thomas, Lady Parsons.

Wincanton Summer Carnival, 1965. On the float, taking a well-earned break from the rigours of the annual summer carnival at Wincanton are: S. Read, C. Rodgers, L. Ansteads, M. Hansford, M. Champion and Irene Clay.

Castle Cary Red Cross, 1951. The Annual Inspection held in Parkers Orchard. Back row, left to right: Tom Moores, Ernie Brewser, Jim Cox, Ron Dunford, Ken Sibbetts, Alex Tiller, Edgar Warr, John Bashford, Vic Chamberlain. In front, left to right: Freddie Biggs, Frank Parker, Bill Thomas, Hubert Laver, Cyril Toop. The cups were awarded to teams from the detachment who entered the county First Aid competition at Yeovil.

To Everything a Season was a presentation of a historical pageant in twelve scenes given in November 1973 at North Cadbury church. This scene depicts the happenings at 'Yarlington Fair' in the late-eighteenth century. In the middle ages Yarlington was granted a charter to hold a great three-day fair. Over the succeeding centuries the fair became more and more important. It was finally abolished in 1900. The actors in this scene include: Russell Kinsey, Edna Lee, John Day, Robert Harvey, Vanda Coulsey, Angus Robson, Christine Wyatt, Tim, Guy and Helen Clothier and Cathy Langdown.

The Great Hall of Camelot. Another scene from the same production and the cast includes: Tony Foottit, Peter Rowe, Neil Bell, Claire Underwood, Stanley Southcombe, David Sparkes, Vanda Coulsey, Christine Wyatt, Angus Robson and Nick Arnott.

Castle Cary town band, 1928. In no particular order are George Weeks, Walter Parsons, Jack Jones, Bill Roper, Fred Hill, Jack Hill, Archie Cooper, George Cooper, George Weeks, Ernie Meadon, Les Elkins, Fred Stockman, Mr Biggin, Bert Hill, Jack Weeks, Archie Creed, Percy Hiscox and Arthur Fox.

Castle Cary parish council. Back row, left to right: John Harrison, George Stockley and Bob Mackie. In the centre row are Guy Churchouse, Tom Biss, Stan Hutchfield, Frank Parker, Jack Otton and Charlie Chilcott. Seated are Percy Boyer, Elizabeth Corp, Jim Garland, Reg Lush and John Bulley.

Castle Cary St John Ambulance on Bailey Hill, *c.* 1947. Left to right: Mrs Harrison, -?-, Maude Cooper, Frances Moore, Jessie Hedditch, Betty Yeabsley, Grace Parsons, Jean Lanning, Jean Talmay, Mollie Bartlett, -?-, Mrs White.

Castle Cary Mother's Union in the 1940s ready for a day out. Among the group are Mrs Newport, Amy Pitman, Mrs Phillips, May Cole, Ella Asher, Granny Goodland, Mrs Hunt, Mrs Poole, Mrs Hearn, Kathleen Corp, Winnie Apsey, Mrs Barber, Mrs Ted Clothier, Mrs Blinman, Lily Poole, Mrs Molesworth, Mrs Ernie White, Mrs Lupton, Lottie Higgins, Rosie Biss, Sister Higgins, Peggy Barratt, Mrs Creed, Mrs Hayward and Revd Lupton.

Prize-giving at Castle Cary, 1910. Some prizes are laid out on the table and the identified men are from left to right: -?-, Dick Creed, H. Collings, W. Chamberlain, David Ash (in the bowler), H. Preter, Walter Barber, -?-, -?-, W. Poole, George Ridout. The message on the reverse of this postcard tells us that W.J. won the case of knives and 'the little man on the left is, well you know who it is'. We don't, neither do we know the occasion!

Red Cross nurses, c. 1943. Red Cross inspection day at the Hollies, Castle Cary. Only people who could be released from work at any time attended Red cross Classes. These nurses acted as duty attendants on the ambulance. Back row, left to right: Mary Cooper, Sylvia Payne, Kath Vicarage, Peggy Dare, Gladys Corp, Violet Pearce. Middle row, left to right: Dorothy Targett, Fanny Mills, Violet Darley (an evacuee from Southampton), Marjorie Bush, Beryl Thomas, Mona Potter and Mrs Lanning. Front row, left to right: Elfreda Perkins, Pam Biss and Joyce Dyas.

Cary Youth Club outing to Brighton, 1955. Wakes No.1 luxury coach, a 26 seater Bedford Duple. Left to right: Robin Wines, Norman Legg, Jean Coombs, Stan Payne, Maureen Stockley, Daphne Yeabsley, Margaret Brine, Ruth Lush, Gerald Brine, Ann Laver, Peter Fletcher, Doug Eades. In the bus is Geoff Ruddle.

Liz white's Dancing Class, c. 1937. Back row, left to right: Betty Close, Margaret Milligan, Hetty Wines, Doreen Brown, Mary Cooper, Betty Whittle. Front row, left to right: Margaret Cave, Edna Whittle, Margaret Whittle and Marian Clothier. These girls from Castle Cary did not pay for their classes but were expected to make a donation which was given to the P.D.S.A. They performed at fetes, garden parties and concerts.

Five

At Work

Ferngrove Farm, Woolston. An albion binder in the oat field has gone wrong.
Mr Herbert Osborn the owner stands with hands on hips as his brother Bill, from Galhampton,
tries to rectify the problem. George Clothier and a workmate offer advice.

The premises of a.F. White of Bruton, 1903. The top photograph shows the cart and waggon works with the covered waggon of T.H. Jennings of Cole Mills, Bruton. (Cole Mill was on the River Brue at Pitcombe). In the bottom picture are members of the White family and their staff at the cycle works with what must have been one of the first cars at Bruton. The three types of transport contrast very well in an age of change. Note the various advertisements in the windows of the cycle works.

Interior of Martins Stores, Castle Cary, 1933. Behind the counter are Sid Appleby and Ernie Ridout. Established in 1875 in South Cary, Martins Stores moved to its present premises in 1917 having already occupied the shop next door since approximately 1890.

A scene taken on Cadbury Castle during the Second World War. Three crops were grown on the summit of the castle in successive years, potatoes, barley and flax but not necessarily in that order. Here the barley straw is being baled and carted. The vehicle on the right is an International Crawler.

Donnes Twine works at Castle Cary. This business was started in 1797 in a small way in cottages at Ansford. By the early 1800s the firm had moved into Cary and quickly built up a reputation of quality goods. Donnes had customers around the world and made a large contribution to the equipment of the three services in both world wars. Twine making was combined at the same premises with the weaving of narrow fabrics. The firm celebrated its 150th anniversary in 1947, and although a family firm for all those years it always moved with the times, using new ideas and new machinery when it became available. The company is still producing quality goods.

B.W. Barrington. Not much is known about this photograph except the obvious and it is included here for its intrinsic value. Benjamin Barrington was a baker at Keinton Mandeville in the years before the First World War.

K. & M. Cox's lorry yard at North Cadbury. The driver is Walter Parker who worked here for many years in the days when the milk churn was 'king'. They have of course now disappeared from the scene in favour of 'bulk milk'. The company moved out of North Cadbury in 1993 and the site was sold for a housing developement.

Squibbs Works at Station Road, Castle Cary, 1904. J.F. Squibb was a coachbuilder, smith and wheelwright. Left to right: Charlie Hill, Walt 'Lightening' Hill, Fox the painter, Bert Hughes, George Squibb, Monty Squibb, Frank Squibb and Jim Squibb.

At dimmer, Castle Cary. Albert Fry and Jim Bartlett loading a trailer on Albert's farm. The cart was made by Bill Vicarage of Yarlington. Note the wooden rake on the back of the trailer.

At Hazlegrove House, Sparkford, c. 1915. These cars belonged to Major Langman (who later became Sir Archibald). One of the drivers is Walter Windsor who was chauffeur to the Langmans. Walter Windsor worked for a time at North Cadbury Court and then for Lord Blackford of Compton Castle as his chauffeur at Whitehall Court in London.

Ferngrove Farm, Woolston, 1930s. Another scene of the farm, this time showing rick-making with elevator and collector. The staff were very likely, Les Arnold, Richard Jeanes, R. Hockey and George Clothier.

The upholstery department at Pithers Emporium, in High Street, Castle Cary.

Above: High Street premises of White's Garage, Bruton, 1929. White's garage, which is now High Street garage was built in 1893. It was taken over by Powell and Rossiter on 23 January 1931 and taken over again by West End garage in August 1953. Here members of the family and staff pose for the camera. The shop on the left was Amor and Sons who were stationers.

Left: Rick-making at Manor Farm, Galhampton. An ingenious system of belts and pullies makes life a little easier for Edward Cornish and his staff.

The blacksmiths at Castle Cary. On the left is Reg Parsons and on the right his father, Alfred Parsons. The family were blacksmiths in Lower Woodcock Street, Castle Cary until fairly recently. They were well-known characters in the town and were excellent craftsmen in wrought ironwork, many examples of their work can be seen locally.

F. PARSONS & SON,
C.S.S.

Shoeing and General Smiths,

Woodcock Street Forge, Castle Cary.

All kinds of Agricultural Machinery repaired.

Lawn Mowers ground by Machinery.

Advertisement for Parsons, 1930.

Above: Charles Goodland with a plough in a field between Clanville Bridge and Alford in 1927. The Goodland family lived in the North Barrow, Alford, Lovington area for several generations.

Left: Lower Ansford Farm, Ansford, home of the Barrett family, 24 October 1936. Many West Country farms made cider from apples grown in their own orchards. The Barretts were no exception.

Squibbs Garage, Castle Cary. The photograph is captioned, 'One Day's Delivery'. The cars were Morris 25, Morris 12-6, Morris 10-4 and Austin 7.

The cabinet-making shop at Pithers Emporium, Castle Cary, 4 May 1906. Three of the men here are George Creed, George Martin and Ted Clothier (the foreman).

Rita Mckerrow in Station Road, Castle Cary. Rita worked for Brakes Dairy whose cart was painted red and yellow. She was a well-known singer who had performed at Glyndbourne. Her grandfather lived in Gas Works Lane. He was the organist at the parish church and was a talented artist and could often be seen around the town with his easel and was always accompanied by his dog.

Some of Pithers' staff outside the office, *c.* 1931. Left to right: B. Newport, M. Clothier, Margaret Pither and Iris Porter.

Premises of E.O. Francis & Sons, smiths and wheelwrights, in Station Road, Castle Cary. Fifth from the right is Oliver Bartlett and also in the picture is George Squibb who later took over the premises. All the men carry a tool of their trade. The cart belonged to Holt Needham of Manor Farm, Castle Cary and is dated 1897. By putting up the sign advertising the *Daily Chronicle* newspaper, the proprietors of the business got a free Sunday paper. In 1875, Edward Oram Francis was a builder and brick and tile-maker on Bailey Hill, Castle Cary.

The canteen staff of Ansford School, 1955. Left to right: Doris Lintern, Kathleen Martin, Mary Smith, Rose Chivers, Peggy Haskins.

The milking staff at Home Farm, North Cadbury, c. 1910. The girl on the left and the girl second from the right are the Lockett sisters who lived at No. 10 High Street, North Cadbury.

Six

Personalities

Polly Hillyer. Mrs Hillyer of North Cadbury outside the post office in Woolston Road. Polly was a familiar sight in North Cadbury and the surrounding villages with her donkey and trap 'taxi'. One story about her is of a trip to Sherborne with passengers bound for the station. On the road at Sigwells a large dog was blocking her way. The donkey would not and did not pass. The only option was to turn round and return home with Polly telling her passengers 'you can go to Sherborne another day'.

Left: W.A. Knight, 1866 to 1949. William Albert Knight was a native of Castle Cary. He was educated at Kings School, Bruton and Battersea Training College. He was appointed headmaster of the Higher Grade School at Maryport in Cumberland when only 22 years old and became head at Sexeys School, Bruton at the age of 24, a post he held until 1927. He was a governor of Sexeys from 1932-1949 and a founder and governor of Sunny Hill Girls School at Bruton, and a governor of the Friends School at Sidcot. He was a pioneer in the development of science teaching in schools. Old Sexeians remembered Mr Knight as both a great headmaster and teacher but above all they remembered him as a friend. He was known to them all as 'Wacker' Knight (but not to his face).

Below: Pither Family. The Pither family at Castle Cary, 20 April 1941. Back row, left to right: Donald, Charles (Cullen) and Denis and in front their brother-in-law William Heath, brother Jonathan (Roy) with his baby son Anthony, and their father John. Donald was invalidated out of the army in 1943 and died in 1944. In his memory the family gave to Castle Cary the 'Donald Pither Memorial Field' to provide a permanent home for the cricket club. Pither & Son Ltd. was started in 1877 by Charles Pither. He was a skilled upholsterer and established a workshop at Castle Cary in premises behind the present library. He also sold china and glassware in what is now Parkers. In the following years the business expanded into removals and storage, cabinet making, furniture making and french polishing. By 1907 the company was trading from premises in High Street with a branch at Bruton. The business expanded further with branches at Yeovil, Wells and Crewkerne. After some years business activities were centred at Crewkerne under the direction of Roy Pither.

Above: Pither Advertisement, January 1936.

Right: W. Macmillan, 1844 to 1911. William Macmillan was known as a kindly, thoughtful, Christian gentleman. He came to Castle Cary in the 1860s and soon founded the Young Men's Society, for the purpose of improving the education and providing healthy amusement for the youths of the town. He was a teetotaller and for a long time led the local Good Templar movement. For 23 years he edited and published a monthly magazine which was known as *The Somerset Vistor.* In 1896 he started publishing *The Cary Visitor* which was a monthly journal combining a chronicle of current events with snippets of local history. Mr Macmillan was also widely known as an antiquary and authority on natural history and was a regular attendant at the annual meetings of the Somerset Archaeological and Natural History Society of which he was a member. He was also a supporter of the Wincanton Field Club. One of his most prized possessions was a valuable collection of moths and butterflies secured almost entirely by his own net. Mr Macmillan's religious work included the duties as secretary of the Zion chapel in South Cary and he was one of the trustees of the church. He started the Adult School at Cary in 1892 and was still its promoter at the time of his death. He was a member of the old school board and a manager of the Council Schools. His other good works included being a governor of Sexey's School at Bruton and committee member of the Wincanton Pensions Board. He was an alderman of the Somerset County Council and JP for Somerset.

Above: Miss Donne. Ethel Florence Donne was the only child of John Stephens Donne of Florida House, Castle Cary. She was married on 8 September 1909 at Castle Cary parish church to Mr P. Courtenay of Weymouth who was a well-known hockey player for his county. The ceremony was performed by the vicar, Revd Wake with Mr McKerrow at the organ. The reception was held at Florida House and a large number of guests were present. The honeymoon or 'wedding tour' as it was called was held in North Wales. This photograph shows the wedding party outside the White Hart in Fore Street.

Right: Mr and Mrs Ford. This couple were well-known at Bayford where they sold lemonade at their cottage door. Note the money box on top of the barrel just in front of the notice giving the price as just one penny (there were 240 pennies to the pound before decimalization).

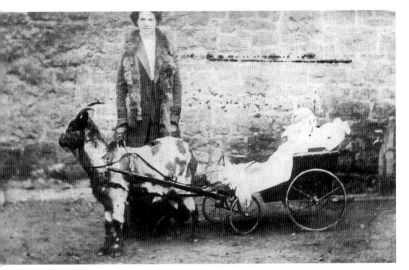

Above: Jack Weeks. The Weeks family lived at the White Hart in Fore Street, Castle Cary for over 70 years. This charming picture is of Jack Weeks and his mother. Mrs Weeks did not have a pram for her son but used this carriage instead. This was intended to be pulled by a dog but she trained a nanny goat to pull it .The carriage harness was made by Mr Biggin of Cary.

Right: Jack Weeks, 1926. Jack, at the age of fourteen outside Hunts Bakery (now Barrington Antiques) in Woodcock Street, Castle Cary. At the time he lived next door. His musical career started with him playing a side drum. He was later taught to play the trombone by Charlie Cooper.

A quadruple purpose sidecar made by a reader of "Motor Cycling." Mr. Ralph Otton, of Castle Cary will be seen that it can be used as a pleasure vehicle, or fitted with a substantial tray, a box carrie with a platform to accommodate bulky goods. The machine is a Premier.

Above left: J.P. Otton, 1909 - 1992. Jack Perceval Otton was born at Castle Cary and lived all his long life in the town. He was educated at Castle Cary School (now the primary school). He was a parish councillor for a period of 38 years, a district councillor for 8 years and a sargeant of police throughout the Second World War. He was in business (electrical, television and radio) with his father and later his son. A member of the Con-stitutional Club, he and two other members saved the club from going bankrupt. There are many tales about Jack, including when he was playing skittles in the Britannia back in the early fifties against the fire service and his team was losing, so he went and called the fire service to Bailey Hill on a false alarm. The game was declared void but Jack Otton went to court and was fined the sum of £20 and bound over to keep the peace. A farmer friend bought a new car from Squibbs Garage and that night the farmer took Jack and five others to North Cadbury. Jack was sat next to the farmer and every corner they went round Jack would nudge the gear stick with his knee and put the car out of gear, consequently the next day the car was traded in for another model. Also, a local butcher once said to Jack in the George Hotel that his trilby hat was the best hat in the town. Whilst the butcher was in the toilet Jack stuck three dart holes through the top of the hat and then Jack made a bet with the butcher that his hat was not waterproof. The butcher emptied a bottle of beer in his hat to prove otherwise. As a choir boy Jack once lit a rocket in the church which went through the nave and made a scorch mark in children's corner. He was once caught in the pulpit by the rector delivering a sermon about the parable 'where the rich man stole the poor mans cabbages and he that sitteth upon a red hot brick shall surely rise again.'

Above right: Otton Advertisement from *Motor Cycling Magazine*, 2 January 1917.

William Arthur Osborn, 1888 – 1975. Mr Osborn was born at Sherborne and came to live at Woolston in the late 1890s. He attended North Cadbury village school and Sexey's at Bruton. On leaving Sexey's he became an apprentice in the electrical engineering trade with Hindleys of Bourton, Dorset. Mr Osborn was a talented musician and played in his regiments band during the First World War and also with the Bourton and Wincanton Bands. He is seen here as a member of the Wincanton Silver Band with the treble and bass trombones. Early in his childhood he learnt the art of bell-ringing and was tower captain at North Cadbury for 45 years. He was very well known over a wide area of the south west of England on account of his knowledge of church bells and church clocks. He married in 1921, Gertrude Cornish of Galhampton, where they lived all their married lives.

George Sweetman. Mr Sweetman was a native and long life resident of Wincanton. His last years were given to collecting archive material of his home town. He started work at the age of 8 years and was a mason by trade until 1862. He was an archaeologist and antiquarian. His early days at Sunday school helped him in his persuit of knowledge and he repaid this by becoming a Sunday school teacher and remaining one for over 40 years. He was also a teetotaller and was faithful to his pledge for over 65 years. His shop in Wincanton marketplace sold many of his pamphlets on the history of Wincanton and books in general on the history of Somerset.

Acknowledgements

Our thanks are due to the many people who have offered help and encouragement to us in this project. Especially we would mention: Roger Otton, Margaret May and the Wincanton Museum, Harold and Marjorie White, Gordon Fry, Jack and Joyce Weeks, Kath Squibb, Mary Mainstone, Colin and Helen Miles, Ted Pendleton, Dick and Judy Bell, Harold and Yvonne Lawrence, David Higgins and Brenda Francis.

Finally we are both very grateful to all those people who have over the years contributed photographs and items of memorabilia to our collections. We would both welcome hearing from anyone who may have anything of interest to add to our knowledge of the area.